LEADERSHIP
IS **DOING**

Pamela J. Newman

Outskirts Press, Inc.
http://www.outskirtspress.com

Paperback ISBN: 978-1-9772-2969-4
Hardback ISBN: 978-1-9772-2971-7

Library of Congress Control Number: 2020913738

Cover Photo © 2020 www.gettyimages.com. All rights reserved - used with permission.

Outskirts Press and the "OP" logo are trademarks belonging to Outskirts Press, Inc.

PRINTED IN THE UNITED STATES OF AMERICA

This book is dedicated to Sari Rudmann,

Chief of Staff at PJN Strategies. She is one of

the people who shows the other people how.

TABLE OF CONTENTS

INTRODUCTION

What generally stops people from being leaders is the fear of doing: People often fear doing. I was surprised when my loving and lovely daughter-in-law, Shannon, recently told me I had said something to her she has found particularly useful to remember. (Shannon is a highly-accomplished private wealth banker by experience and a highly-effective wife and mother of three wonderful children.) I had to wonder what I could have said to her that she would have found so compelling.

"Shannon", I said, "What did I say?" She said, "You told me that people often don't do things; make things happen, create change and deliver results because they fear getting started "doing".

I had to laugh when Shannon said this to me. In fact, I was told this by Shannon while visiting her in La Jolla, CA. Actually, the trip to nearby San Diego had started to seem overwhelming to me to consider taking in the days before the departure from New York City. I had started to see real and imagined obstacles to making the trip. For example, I didn't think I could wake up early enough in the morning both to conduct my required exercise program and catch an 8am flight out of JFK Airport. Who would take care of my dog, Mandarin Joey, and my cat, Champagne Buttercup? Could I afford to be away from my work responsibilities?

Fortunately, I stopped thinking about the trip and started executing it. I selected, and sent by mail, the gifts for the grandchildren. I woke up an hour earlier than usual on the day of departure and easily did my routine exercise program before departing for the airport. I picked projects I hadn't tackled but needed to do (like finishing writing this book) to take with me and work on while on the plane. I started organizing for the trip and was now on the trip.

This personal and simple description of taking a family trip to see people I greatly love in a town that some consider paradise might not strike you as the apotheosis of leadership. However, it is a good story for understanding that leadership is doing. Doing begets doing. Doing begets leadership.

Also, a hard thing to do is to write a book on leadership that works for everyone. It is hard to think of what I want to write about, how to say it and then, to sit down and write it. Like planning and executing a trip, the thinking about what to say and write often slows down and even stops the execution of writing the book. It is so much easier to find something else to do than write a book.

Once I have made a plan for a book, like making a plan for a trip, the execution of the plan is both manageable and enjoyable. Leaders like to make things happen.

This book is a series of short vignettes about moments of leadership as defined as moments of doing.

I decided on this topic of leadership because, as a Civilian Aide to the Secretary of the Army (CASA) for the South Region of New York, I have been fascinated by the outstanding capability of the U.S. Army to instill the concept of "doing" into the Army citizen. Some people describe this as discipline; others describe it as being prepared. I describe the "doing" as the backbone of what leadership is about. Leaders are people who are trained how to do, cultivate "doing" in their lives and, when they find themselves in extraordinary circumstances, are able to execute what becomes known as acts of heroism.

My other daughter-in-law, Mary, also demonstrated the meaning of "leadership is doing" when we found ourselves in a family squabble. "Come" she said to all of us. "Let's form the friendship of love circle and then we can work out this dispute." This simple act of leadership of getting a loving family huddling and hugging each other took the prickle out of the discussion and allowed a rational game plan to be in place. Mary is not only beautiful and loving; she is a doer, a leader.

Please enjoy the simple, but powerful vignettes that support the theme and title of this book "Leadership Is Doing".

VISUALIZE THE OUTCOME

I recently met with Dr. Gary Wiren, one of the most heralded and respected professionals in the world of golf. Gary earned a Master's Degree from the University of Michigan and a Doctorate from the University of Oregon in Sports Science.

Gary believes in the power of visualization.

I concur with Gary's thinking about visualization: As a child, in Kalamazoo, Michigan, I visualized myself living in an apartment in New York City. I had no idea what an apartment in New York City looked like. I had no reason to think I would ever live in New York City. I, in fact, had never been to New York City. Yet, I have lived these last several decades in a wonderful apartment in the middle of New York City.

The outcome I visualized was achieved.

REFUSE TO TOLERATE PREJUDICE

Every time we are with others and hear a racial, ethnic or religious slur, I suggest we interrupt the conversation and say, *"I am not comfortable with denigrating any group or any individual."*

We are living, at the writing of this book, in an era where racial and religious incidents in the United States have more than doubled over one year ago. Places of worship have seen a flurry of active shooter events. Schools, retail stores and entertainment centers now must think about how to protect their environment from hate mongers.

We can never forget our American principle of equality. We must practice the premise of equality always. We must speak out when people ignore the basic premise of equality.

I recently had a fun and funny experience: I was having my regular Christmas Eve dinner at a restaurant with the Wangs. Ed Wang was born in America. His wife, the beautiful Sophia, was born in China. Their two children, Ed Jr. and Alexander, have been in my life since they were very young.

A man at a neighboring table from ours walked over to our table. He had clearly observed how tight knit we were as a unit. He asked, "Are you a family?"

"Yes, indeed, we are!" Ed responded without hesitating.

The man shook his head at us while he tried to absorb how incredulous this concept was for him. After he left our table, Ed looked at me and said the obvious, "By now, we are family."

Families, Ed realized, are no longer simply based on blood lines. Prejudice is simply out of date for who we are today.

STAND UP FOR WHAT IS CORRECT

A remarkable story is told about standing up for what is correct in the book, *G.I. Jews*, authored by Deborah Dash Moore. The book tells the story of about 500 American prisoners of war who were put in a prisoner of war camp in Germany during World War II. A German officer in charge of the prisoner of war camp told the American battalion leader in charge of the 500 U.S. soldiers that he needed to have all the Jewish American soldiers at the camp ready and lined up the next morning for "removal".

The battalion commander, though painfully young and himself a Protestant, instead, lined up all 500 soldiers in his battalion the next morning. When the German officer saw everybody lined up in the whole prisoner of war camp, he implored the battalion commander "Why didn't you line up just the eleven Jewish soldiers as I so ordered you?"

The American battalion commander responded "Sir. We are all Jews". With that response, the German officer took his pistol and placed it right on the forehead of the U.S. battalion commander. He then said to him, "I'm going to blow off your head and everyone else's in this camp". The battalion commander may have flinched, but his answer came quickly: "Sir, you can murder me and these 500 American prisoners of war, but the war is about over and this action of you killing me and 500 others will mean that my country will hunt you down and make <u>you</u> a prisoner of war.

The German officer reluctantly dropped his gun and walked away.

The battalion commander never talked about this extraordinary feat of courage when he returned home to the Midwest. Until the author of the book, *G.I. Jews*, did her research, this story was not well known.

I would like to see a blog where people report on the blog stories about people who do things because it is the correct thing to do. Doing the correct thing takes courage, extra energy, perseverance, risk taking and a fundamental belief that "right is right".

PUT YOUR OWN NEEDS ASIDE

David Fitzgerald, a friend and decorated Army Veteran, told me that although he was a recipient of the Bronze Star Medal, he never let his own ego become more important than his practice of caring about his soldiers first and foremost. He described the story of a soldier in Iraq getting first lost and then ultimately kidnapped by the Taliban and eventually found dead. While the soldier was not part of David's battalion, he says he is still haunted daily by wondering what happened that allowed a soldier, any soldier, from having had this ever happen.

David points out that the Army constantly attempts to improve how they do things by conducting an "After Action Review," which is a step-by-step examination of what happened on every engagement. David says that, to this day, even in his civilian life, he says to himself: *"Am I doing everything that I am supposed to be doing? My number one thing to do is think more about others than myself. Once you put your own needs aside, you can become more effective at what you are doing. My Dad taught me to feed my "troops" before I feed myself."*

Thinking about others first is a great way to:

1) reduce depression.

2) create purpose.

3) give back.

4) improve what gets done.

PLAN WHAT YOU NEED TO DO

David Fitzgerald, a good friend, who spent thirty years in the U.S. Army, (who I talk about in Axiom #4), taught me a phrase about the importance of planning which I have never forgotten:

"Proper prior planning prevents poor performance."

The importance of planning cannot be overemphasized. Here are a few suggested tips on planning I strongly endorse.

1. **Write Down the What/When/How of Your Plan**
   I just bought a ten-year calendar. I want my calendar, for the next ten years, to reflect my goals and objectives for the next ten years. If my goal is to be more physically fit, then my calendar should reflect a great deal of inserts to reserve time for exercise.

2. **Have the Right Tools/Supplies/Equipment to Execute Your Plan**
   Anyone who travels frequently learns and applies the principles of planning to travel. The frequent traveler knows preparation for travel requires having a collection of luggage so that the size of the suitcase is compatible with the length of the trip. She knows to have essentials organized for travel such as electrical plugs for

different countries, cords for phones and tablets, prescriptions and backup eyeglasses.

I keep a list of frequently needed travel supplies that I always consult and take with me when I travel. My list includes my:

- Date of Trip: _____

- Location: _____

- Special Needs: _____

- Passport

- Ticket

- Boarding Pass

- Itinerary

- Back up printed copy of my passport

- Contact lenses and an extra pair of contact lenses

- Glasses

- Phone Chargers

- Cords for tablets and phones

- Medications/First Aid Items

- Electric plugs

- Life goals and my ten-year calendar

- Hand Sanitizers

- Masks

- Gloves

Even when not traveling, I make a weekly list describing:

- What am I going to wear every day that week?
- Where I am going to have dinner each night of the week?
- What I want to discuss in the many conversations I expect to have each week. I actually prepare an agenda and send it ahead of time to the person, or people, with whom I am meeting for every appointment. A sample agenda is on the next page:

DRAFT AGENDA

Date: October 1, 2020

Time: 10:00AM

Location: Office of PJN Strategies LLC
             870 United Nations Plaza
             Suite 33C
             New York, NY 10017
             (212) 980-3435

Attendees:

PJN Strategies LLC
Pamela J. Newman, President and CEO
David J. Katz, Managing Director

XYZ Company
_____, President
_____, CFO

Discussion Items:

- Tell me about your business?
- What obstacles do you face?
- How can we help you go and grow?

Next Steps:

I plan over the course of ten years:

- What I can do for others.

- Trips I want to take.

- Family excursions and events.

- Dinner parties.

- Subjects I want to study.

- Changes in my behavior I want to make.

A chart below gives examples of these plans:

Under-taking	Example	Obstacle	Action
Trips to Take	Israel	How to learn as much as possible while there about the history of Israel	Selecting an AIPAC trip last November where lectures and learning opportunities were provided morning, afternoon and evening
Family Excursions	My "Big Birthday"	Selecting a date the whole family could be there	Not letting my actual birthday date stand in the way of the goal of the whole family being there

Under-taking	Example	Obstacle	Action
Study	Learning the history of Israel	Have the time to read twelve books on Israel	I downloaded seven of the twelve books I obtained on my audio app and listened to them while exercising

Some of the most useful life planning I have done is listed below:

1. **Planning for years 60 – 100.** Our schools do not spend enough time helping people realize that their lives might outlast their money, their health and their family. Plans and backup plans reduce the stress of managing this stage of life. Chuck Stetson has taught me the goal of "squaring the curve," which means having every decade of life get better than the previous one; live until you are 100 and simply die one night in your sleep.

2. **Planning your funeral and burial site.** Creating your will, bequeathing of possessions, and memorializing funeral and burial preferences reduces family stress and uncertainty.

3. **Taking advantage of resources that mitigate life interruption.** How would you pay your bills if you lost your job? How would you manage long-term care for you and/or a family member?

Planning, as a leadership tool, is a major differentiator of people who let life happen to them instead of having their lives match their dreams.

LEADERS COMPREHEND

When COVID-19 knocked on everybody's door in early 2020, it was an event that demobilized many people. On the other hand, it was an event that galvanized a certain amount of people into performing helpful solutions. Hospital workers, first responders, food supply workers all made the Coronavirus less of a panic than it might have been.

A person who did more than his fair share, reducing the uncertainty and fear of the financial consequence of COVID-19, is my colleague, David Katz. As soon as the government created the Paycheck Protection Program, David was quick to get to clients, colleagues and friends with helpful and important knowledge and a willingness to enable people to benefit from this program.

David's amazing ability to absorb the knowledge of what the program would allow, and not allow, and translate that into an appropriate application was simply remarkable.

THE VALUE OF
THE MENTOR/PROTÉGÉ RELATIONSHIP

A great way to measure where you are on the scale of being a true leader is to ask and answer for yourself this question: *"How many protégés am I mentoring?"*

Implicit in leadership talent is the ability to persuade other people to follow you.

I have had, over the last couple of years, the opportunity to be a protégé to an outstanding leader. When I became a Civilian Aide to the Secretary of the Army, I truly had very little concept of how to perform this important function. Wonderful William (Bill) Murdy (former CASA – Connecticut) reached out to me and asked me if he could guide and educate me on the responsibilities of being a Civilian Aide to the Secretary of the Army. Bill is a West Point graduate and has had an incredibly successful career as a leader in business.

I have taken pleasure in watching how well Bill navigates me and improves my skill sets. What I specifically noticed was that he did three things:

1. **Bill took the time to evolve me.** Leaders recognize that if you are going to get people to

follow your thinking, it's a significant time investment. Bill took the time out of his own schedule to meet with me and introduce me to various aspects of the Army. In our first visit, he helped me understand what the Army Corps of Engineers does. In the next visit, what the Head of Public Relations for the Army is about. After each meeting, with various units of the Army, Bill debriefed me about what we had learned from that branch of the Army.

2. **Bill Murdy displays the incredible focus it takes to be a leader.** A leader captures people, captures the room, and captures the entire environment he or she is occupying. He or she listens intently and nods as he or she absorbs what I am saying. As he or she learns the information I am sharing, he or she registers comprehension with frequent commentary and acknowledgement.

Leaders practice their capacity to focus. When they make an introduction, they hold their eye contact just slightly longer than customary. In conversations they keep their eyes glued to the eyes of the other person. Leaders lean into other people. Leaders reflect in facial cues that they hear the other person. One of the highest compliments I ever received was from a woman name Dinny Monroe who said to me *"You listen like what you are hearing is the missing link to the final equation".* Leaders focus on listening.

3. **Bill Murdy has an open way.** He doesn't see a reason to build walls in a relationship. Transparency is critical. Not only do leaders talk about their families and their children, they also talk about their vacation plans, their retirement plans and their plans for the weekend. Leaders are not afraid for their protégés to see their foibles and their failings. By being vulnerable, they remarkably gain leadership respect.

LEADERS INSPIRE OTHERS

Recently, I had a need to be a leader: I wanted to motivate an orthopedic surgeon, an anesthesiologist, and a surgical nurse to be committed to the success of the surgery they needed to do on my broken humerus bone. Being inspiring while wearing a blue head cap and an open-on-the-backside hospital gown is, indeed, a daunting task. Nevertheless, I straightened my backbone and gave a speech to all three professionals in the operating room about how confident I was that they had the talent and commitment to successfully conduct the surgery ahead of us to mend my broken arm.

You might argue that the speech I made caused no difference in the outcome of my healing. You might argue that professionals don't need pep talks. But every time I throw a ball or zip up my dress, with great ease, I'm inclined to think that my motivational speech is what makes my arm work so well!

RECOGNIZE WHAT YOUR POSITION MEANS

Roosevelt Giles, Chairman of The Atlanta Life Insurance Company, recently described to us a meeting where his listeners were pretty demanding. I asked Roosevelt how he kept his always cool demeanor while being confronted. Roosevelt responded: *"You just have to take it".*

I have done an informal study of characteristics of great leaders: A common theme I have noted is the leader's ability to remain unscarred and undeterred by criticism. Leaders recognize the truth in the quote *"Have you ever seen a statue of a critic?"*

Michael Bloomberg, founder of Bloomberg and former Mayor of New York City, used the significant setback of being fired as the motivator that compelled him to build a tremendous company.

Gilda Radner achieved a career of being one of the funniest world performers after a college professor suggested to her that she limit her expectations and stick to performing in children's theatre productions.

Achieving a protective skin that is insensitive to questioning critics is, and of itself, an art form. Ways to develop a protective skin include:

1. Determine the validity of the criticism and if you believe it is valid consider the knowledge gained as a huge gift.

2. Ask yourself what does the critic actually understand about what you are trying to do.

3. Keep a list of famous people whose work was originally objected to and described as not good enough. CK Rowland could not get any publisher to accept <u>Harry Potter</u> for publication for several years.

4. Appreciate the lessons learned by people who are military leaders: The military teaches their leaders to endure ignominy and embarrassment in recognition of achieving a higher goal for their team.

5. Start the next day with the criticism that was leveled at you as a thing of the past. Dwelling on yesterday's setbacks, defeats and criticisms is futile. Remember *"Yesterday is a cancelled check".*

6. A leader looks like a leader and behaves like a leader. Roosevelt Giles' ever-cool demeanor in the face of criticism is a level of leadership that would make General George Patton proud.

Countenance is the appearance a person puts forward. A leader listens, talks, acts, breathes and thinks like a leader. This is why you know a leader when you see one.

A leader wakes up in the morning recognizing the responsibilities of being a leader. A leader executes on their responsibilities all day long.

LEADERS INSPIRE

True leaders inspire. People gravitate to them and look to them for guidance for better ideas and brilliant thoughts that can guide their own lives.

True leaders exemplify:

- *"It Can Be Done"* thinking (a plaque President Reagan kept in the Oval Office).

- The willingness to do anything that they ask their followers to do.

- The ability to create the opportunity for their followers to become more than they are.

- A high tolerance for people who may not yet do a task well enough but clearly want to get better.

- Joy in the day, the task, the challenge.

- The ability to get back into the center of the ring after a setback or failure.

- Giving credit to others for jobs well done.

- A desire to learn.

LEADERSHIP MOMENTS ARE DERIVED FROM A COLLECTION OF SHORT EVENTS.

It is important to recognize that leaders are made as a result of many short events. Recognizing leadership comes in episodes is a critical observation because people frequently assume being a leader is derived from a long and sustained event.

While it is possible for someone to become a leader as a result of managing a sustained event, it is actually more likely a leader will be made from many short events over a period of time. A good example of this is Dr. Harris Pastides, who, until recently, was the President of the University of South Carolina.

Dr. Pastides is nearly universally acclaimed as a great leader in the community of higher education. Some of the features of his administration reinforced the point that leadership is born out of a succession of remembered moments about him. Students found Dr. Pastides was always available to talk to them. His availability and quiet mentoring of a student was, to the young person, much like finding oil is to a driller. His time, his sage thinking, his kindness was noted. His ten-minute talks with his students were treasured.

Faculty and staff benefited from this same availability

of being able to sit down with Dr. Pastides for a quiet discussion. Since Dr. Henry Kissinger pointed out that universities are often more political than the political climate of Washington, D.C., his availability to discuss with the faculty and administration their concerns and criticisms greatly improved the climate of the University.

Dr. Pastides enjoyed the fun of a campus community. He showed up at school events.

Education is to Dr. Pastides what oxygen is to a living organism. Education is what keeps him going and growing.

To Dr. Pastides, his work is his "calling". Great leaders do not have jobs …. they have missions grounded in purpose.

LEADERSHIP IS ABOUT CHANGE OF BEHAVIOR

Anthony Lucidi was given a seemingly impossible task by a client. He was asked to put forward social media that would change the way people thought about his client.

Instead of seeing the client as limited and controlling information, Anthony developed a campaign to explain how this client's services were socially responsible and useful to the business economy. Anthony, as a technology pro, knows that you can use sound messaging to:

- Teach.

- Better define what people are doing.

- Help people see the other side of an issue.

Anthony is not only fluid on the technology tools of today, he is also exceptional at his capacity to reframe how people think about something.

THE U.S. ARMY TEACHES PEOPLE HOW TO BE LEADERS

When I became a Civilian Aide to the Secretary of the Army on October 20, 2017, I had no idea it would be an experience so enriching, fascinating and important. Being a Civilian Aide to the Secretary of the Army (CASA) has been an exhilarating experience because I have been able to see, firsthand, how this organization teaches people how to be leaders.

The first leadership experience I witnessed was the October 20, 2017 Investiture at The Pentagon of my appointment. The event was more formal than both of my weddings combined. It was also elegant and profound.

Acting Secretary Ryan D. McCarthy conducts the
investiture of Pamela J. Newman on October 20, 2017*

My day-long visit to the Pentagon was chock-a-block with introductions, meetings, completing paperwork and education sessions. At each session, I observed true leadership in action. Each person I met was carrying out his or her stated purpose with passion and focus.

Each person I met with at the Pentagon impressed on me that my responsibility as a Civilian Aide is to "Tell The Army Story". That said, as a Civilian Aide, I am given wide latitude as to what "The Army Story" is and to whom I can tell it.

Since becoming a Civilian Aide to the Secretary of the

---

* Ryan D. McCarthy was confirmed by the U.S. Senate, Sept 26, 2019, and sworn in as the 24th Secretary of the U.S. Army, Sept 30, 2019. McCarthy was unanimously confirmed by the U.S. Senate and appointed as the 33rd Under Secretary of the Army.

Army for New York South, I think I have told "The Army Story", as I see it, to well over two thousand people. I talk about "The Army Story" with colleagues, clients, family members, people next to me on planes and trains, not-for-profit organizations, students, teachers, executives, politicians, researchers and academics.

What I tell people is that:

1. The Army teaches people how to be leaders.

2. Few Americans truly understand what soldiers in Iraq, Iran, Yemen and Afghanistan have experienced which is the need to become a leader of a team on the battlefield.

3. The Army strives to get better at teaching leadership development every day. The Army challenges their own underlying assumptions to ever self-improve leader-making skills.

4. People who are "Army" respect each other. Respect for others is a core leader behavior.

LEADERS HELP OTHERS DO BETTER

I recently asked Dr. Charles Flynn if he could help me get across "The Army Story" to his students. Dr. Flynn, President of the College of Mount Saint Vincent in New York City, quickly warmed to a meeting with Lt. Col. Juddson C. Floris, Ms. Amanda Hay-Carrofino and me. As he learned from us how the Army could benefit his students, he jumped on board as to how to use the Army as a tool for his students to become more than they would otherwise be. After our meeting, Dr. Flynn sent me the following email:

From: Charles Flynn

Sent: Wednesday, August 08, 2018 6:13 PM

To: Pamela Newman

Dear Pamela,

Good meeting today. Thank you for getting us together. We can significantly improve what we are accomplishing in this area.

Charles

Dr. Flynn recognized that the Army can, and does, facilitate a core value of his and the College of Mount St. Vincent: *"We must all help others do better!"*

RESPECT YOUR LEADER

I would like to go back and re-read the book "The Caine Mutiny", authored by Herman Wouk. Like many other books I have re-read, I find that, as I become older, my point of view about a book changes. For example, when I first read "The Devil Wears Prada", I thought Miss Priestly was a ghastly and difficult boss. As time went by, I re-read the book and appreciated this character, Miss Priestly, was demanding but able to teach young people what it meant to "reach".

I also re-read Arthur Miller's "Death of a Salesman". Willy Loman, seen through my youthful eyes, is an unattractive, boorish salesman. Reread as an experienced adult and long-time salesperson, Willy Loman looks like an upright and reliable citizen finding positivity in all he does. Despite his positivity and reliability, the son of his long-time client eyes him with disrespect, skepticism and the message "You are an old and unnecessary person."

In the "The Caine Mutiny", we, the readers, are horrified by Captain Queeg's apparent unnecessary quirky particulars. His distribution of strawberries to the sailors on the boat seemed ludicrous. It is not until after the mutiny, and at the end of the court martial, that we are allowed to understand the fundamental important reliability of a man whose consistent striving

for standards should be viewed as useful rather than
bizarre.

Greenwald, who was the lawyer for the court martial
of Captain Queeg, comments:

> "Well, sure, you guys all have mothers, but
> they wouldn't be in the same bad shape mine
> would if we'd of lost this war, which of course
> we aren't, we've won the damn thing by now.
> See, the Germans aren't kidding about the Jews.
> They're cooking us down to soap over there.
> They think we're vermin and should be 'stermi-
> nated and our corpses turned into something
> useful. Granting the premise – being warped, I
> don't, but granting the premise, soap is as good
> an idea as any. But I just can't cotton to the idea
> of my mom melted down into a bar of soap. I
> had an uncle and an aunt in Cracow, who are
> soap now, but that's different, I never saw my
> uncle and aunt, just saw letters in Jewish from
> them, ever since I was a kid, but never could
> read them. Jew, but I can't read Jewish.
>
> Of course, we figured in those days, only fools
> go into the armed service. Bad pay, no mil-
> lionaire future, and you can't call your mind or
> body your own. Not for sensitive intellectuals.
> So, when all hell broke loose and the Germans
> started running out of soap and figured, well
> it's time to come over and melt down old Mrs.
> Greenwald – who's going to stop them? Not

her boy Barney. Can't stop a Nazi with a law-
book. So, I dropped the lawbooks and ran to
learn how to fly. Stout fellow. Meantime, and
it took a year and a half before I was any good,
who was keeping Mama out of the soap dish?
Captain Queeg."

Young people often do not have the lenses to see how their reactions are narrow because they have not yet had the experiences that demonstrate why you respect your leader.

LEADERS UNDERSTAND THE POWER OF PURPOSE

I visited Howard Schlesinger today. Howard is a terrific architect and real estate developer in New York City. Howard discussed with me his fundamental modus operandi, which is life about purpose.

Richard Stone often lectures teachers and students. He talks about the importance of determining "what is your calling"? He wants people to "authentically reset" their capability from "to **have,** to **do,** and to **be"** so that the priority is instead "to **be,** to **do** and to **have."** He comments that people who are able to do this recognize that happiness is the ultimate syncing of vocation and avocation.

In Israel, almost everybody serves in the military at some point in their life. Higher purpose, the respect for, and to, their country, is ingrained in each Israeli soldier.

LEADERS REACT TO SOCIAL CHANGE

A wonderful spokesman for the U.S. Army came to visit me. Gary Port is the Ambassador for New York for the United States Army Reserve. The nuggets of knowledge Ambassador Port shared with me are very useful.

Ambassador Port sees the Army as an "engine of social change." He points out that the Army has been a front runner on achieving diversity of religion and race and gender. Regardless of the physical limitations, the Army has managed well the socialization of diverse people without interrupting the quality of the mission getting achieved.

LEADERS DO MORE THAN LISTEN

Lots of people listen very well. They "ahah" "ahah" very nicely and they nod sympathetically.

Having listened well, very few people do something to help the individual who is dealing with a frustration, grievance or remembered pain.

Richard Colton exemplifies taking responsibility once he listens. He sees taking corrective action as a key element of the process of good listening skills. I will never forget how capably Richard managed to reduce a concern I had, by going back to the other individual involved without my knowing it. He shared with that person my concerns and suggested to that individual what action that person could take to alleviate my concerns. That action will always be, for me, an unforgettable moment of appreciation for one of Richard Colton's many talents.

LEADERSHIP MEANS GETTING UP AGAIN AFTER FALLING DOWN

Recently, I attended "The Clambake" Dinner for The American University for Financial Services. The school gave their important *Great American Award* to General David H. Petraeus.

After he was introduced, General Petraeus delivered a cogent and powerful speech.

General Petraeus explained:

1) Everyone fails. The trick, he pointed out, is in being able to get up again after failure.

2) People will overlook mistakes and setbacks if they see humility and effort.

3) Life happens quickly. Recover from falling down.

Petraeus quoted Theodore Roosevelt's timely words:

"It is not the critic who counts; not the man who points out how the strong man stumbles, or where the doer of deeds could have done better. The credit belongs to the man who is actually in the arena; whose face is marred by dust and sweat and blood; who strives valiantly; who errs and comes short again and again; who knows the great enthusiasm, the great devotions and spends himself in a worthy cause; who at the best knows in the end the triumph of high achievement; and who at the worst, if he fails at least fails while daring greatly; so that his place shall never be with those cold and timid souls who know neither victory nor defeat."

General Petraeus recognizes that true leadership is about the person who can get up after being knocked down.

RESPECT IS AN ART FORM

My work as a Civilian Aide to the Secretary of the Army reinforces for me three important concepts of respect:

1. The history of our country is important for everyone to learn about.

2. Our flag needs to be honored. Our flag symbolizes the values of our country.

3. The protocols and practices of other countries must be understood, studied and appreciated.

Respect is premised on certain platforms, such as:

- **Age merits respect.** Irving Shapiro pointed out "You cannot put an old head on young shoulders". The experiences of someone's life merits respect.

- **Title merits respect.** Someone who has achieved a professional title merits respect for having obtained a higher standard of knowledge.

- **Achievement merits respect.** We must acknowledge achievement. Veterans have achieved experience at keeping us safe. Veterans merit respect.

- **<u>Clients and customers merit respect.</u>** When people spend their money on us, they deserve our respect for doing so.

The Army teaches its soldiers and officers to have and demonstrate respect. People in the Army learn to have respect and demonstrate respect in a variety of ways. They:

- Listen intently to others.

- Address others as "Sir" and "Ma'am".

- Believe punctuality is a demonstration of respect for others.

- Realize appearance creates respect.

- Strive for higher rank to be deserved of respect.

- Understand that meritocracy garners respect.

Army citizens interject into their conversation positive nodding, quiet responsive acknowledgements and queries, excellent mid-discussion and end-of-discussion summaries.

PEOPLE NEVER FORGET LEADERS

The Five Star General, Douglas MacArthur, borrowed these words for his remarks before the United States Congress on April 19, 1951 for his Farewell Address:

He said: *"Old Soldiers Never Die, They Just Fade Away".*

People, like General MacArthur, who are brilliant at their career are always remembered and always appreciated. Regardless of what profession you think about, it is pretty easy to come up with one or two legends in that space. By definition, a legend never disappears. A legend is someone who has exhibited superlative capabilities over a considerable period of time. General Douglas MacArthur was emblematic of what every soldier wants to be. He was courageous, he was serious. He led with heart. He inspired his soldiers to do better than they ever thought they could do.

He believed the impossible could be achieved and he succeeded in achieving the impossible.

LEADERS HAVE EXCELLENT COMMUNICATION SKILLS

If you talk to a member of the Army, you might get a firm warm salute and direct eye contact as you say "Hello" and throughout your conversation. The Army soldier speaks clearly, firmly and respectfully.

These behaviors, of the U.S. Army citizen, lead me to think we need to help the rest of our society operate to this high military standard. I notice people on the street today rarely make eye contact. People get on buses, subways and trains and do not acknowledge fellow passengers. People get on elevators and don't acknowledge other people in the elevator.

If people had the opportunity to learn, from the Army, communication standards, we would likely find:

- Honking would be nonexistent.

- Driving accidents would be cut down by a third because people would put courtesy over selfishness.

- People would regularly say "Hello" to each other on the street.

- Everybody would share with each other the ethos of "How may I help you today?"

- People would complain less often.

- Excitement for our interpersonal relationships would create health, educational and business benefits.

Communication is something almost everyone does unevenly well. The Army citizen does communication very well and often brilliantly.

THROUGH COMMUNITY LEADERSHIP, WE COULD ELIMINATE LITTER

I wonder if there is a way a U.S. citizen could use Army standards to engage in the mission of no more litter in the U.S. This is a bold initiative. Our country, for no reason I understand, has become tolerant of litter. Why?

I saw negligible litter when I visited Denmark. The canals in Copenhagen were as fresh as a salmon farm. I saw no dirty tissue on the subways in Japan. I watched the curbs and streets of Paris being cleaned each evening with gentle steams of water.

In the United States of America, however, there is nothing unusual about litter on sidewalks, in streets and in shopping malls. Our public garbage cans are often overflowing with garbage. Our streets and sidewalks are often strewn with litter. Graffiti has become commonplace.

Uncollected garbage on the streets of our major cities is unattractive to look at and unpleasant to smell.

Could we, I wonder, use Army methodology to:

- Develop an "End Litter Campaign"?

- Assign resources to create a timetable and action plan to eliminate litter?

- Evolve a program where citizens throughout the U.S. pitch in and do their fair share to eliminate litter?

Think about it: You cannot go to an Army base, West Point or any Army facility and see litter. Why?

It is almost 2021 and our society has never been more environmentally responsible. We have never been more cognizant of the relationship between germs, litter and disease. Inexplicably, we have never had more litter around us.

Let's not wait for the government to fix a problem we can manage to fix quite well ourselves.

LEADERS KNOW SMALL ACTS ARE AS IMPORTANT AS LARGE ONES

John (Jack) Morris is a distinguished servant of the United States Army. He served as an enormous business leader. He is active in philanthropic causes. His large gestures to improve our world are many and valued.

Not only is Jack a master of the major endeavors but he is brilliant at knowing even the smallest things matter. Not only did Jack, and his wonderful wife, Cristine, attend my husband's funeral in New York City, but they were two of the very few people who also volunteered to drive four hours to Providence, Rhode Island to attend a memorial service on my husband's behalf as well.

I will never forget this small, but incredibly meaningful, act of time and caring generosity Jack gave to me.

LEADERS CAN REDUCE THE DRUG EPIDEMIC

The Army and other military branches do a magnificent job fighting wars and protecting our country. I am concerned we need to deploy the expertise and ingenuity of the Army to help resolve a very real problem of our society: One hundred fifteen people a day die in the United States from opioid overdose. We are losing more people a year from this problem than from all the soldiers that died in the Vietnam War.

Could our citizens set the goal of eradicating death from opioid overdosing?

Could we:

1. Identify where there are "hot spots" of opioid overdose in the United States?

2. Develop methodologies to get people off their opioid dependency.

3. Establish places and programs that heighten rehab success?

4. Establish monitoring programs? and

5. Assign "citizen soldiers" to help citizens in need?

The opioid crisis in the United States is a very real enemy. Our highly capable citizens need to recognize that the enemy, opioid overdosing, needs to be snuffed out. An entire country (as we saw happen to China during the late 19th century and early 20th century depicted in the movie "The Last Emperor") can be brought down to its knees from drug overuse.

In today's society, we understand where the enemy is and who the enemy is. Drug overdose is the enemy as it challenges productivity, destroys families and limits innovation. The skills of our citizens need to be applied to Enemy Number One: Opioid Addiction.

VETERANS HOSPITALS STRIVE TO HEAL PEOPLE

How could I have missed it? Just twenty blocks from where I live, on a street named "Veterans Hospital Way", is a block-long building which houses *The Veterans Hospital - NY Harbor Healthcare System in New York City.*

I arrived, last year, at The Veterans Hospital, at the appointed time for a scheduled private tour. As a Civilian Aide to the Secretary of the Army, (CASA), New York Region, I have the honor of being able to tour Army entities in New York City and to provide feedback on what I observed to the Secretary of the Army in a "Significant Activities Report".

I was greeted by Claude Benjamin, Public Affairs Specialist. This beautiful and stylish grandmother is an inveterate New Yorker who gives to her community as a way of life. Ms. Benjamin was a Chinese Studies major at Columbia University, which certainly demonstrates that she has the ability to grasp and command the difficult. By the end of our tour, I could see that Ms. Benjamin had not only the ability to grasp a difficult assignment, but the capacity to wrestle the matter to a useful outcome.

I came to understand, her talent, was characteristic of the capabilities of the staff of this important Veterans

Hospital. To a person, the people I met at this Veterans Hospital were passionate about their work purpose, at the top of their game technically, and eager to make sure people understand the value of their institution.

In the "Gait Lab", I watched how a biomedical engineer, a physical therapist and an orthopedic doctor work collaboratively to help veterans have a prosthesis device fit appropriately.

In the Women's Clinic, I witnessed how women are able to get gender-knowledgeable women's care in an environment that is designed to be friendly to discussing sensitive issues.

The astonishing observation was my chance to visit "The Clubhouse". It is regularly open to all veterans, but on every Thursday, women veterans have one side to themselves. Under the fine leadership of Anthony Stamatouras, the women I spoke with in this room rely on "The Clubhouse" as a way to improve their mental health. This is a room where people gain strength to stay sober, reject drugs and overcome their pain-searing memories for cathartic relief. The only thing I could see that was wrong with this room was that it needed to be 24/7/52 available to our veterans. People who have served our country at all hours get low at all hours, so we need to accommodate their pain at all hours.

In "The Clubhouse", John Tatarakis, CNS, Local Recovery Coordinator, delivered a powerful presentation on what "The Clubhouse" is about and why it exists. His comment about the importance of purpose for mental health recovery registered. When an individual serves our country with a clearly defined mission of putting himself or herself in life and death situations every single day, it's then a challenge to transition to the broader, less-defined responsibilities of family, work and community. The Veterans Hospital provides a supportive environment to reconnect with other veterans. Absence of purpose is a problem for many people. Absence of purpose for a military veteran is an elevated level of a large societal schism. "The Clubhouse" members know this schism and value that those on either side of them "get it" as well.

Veteran programs in New York City are wonderfully promoted to veterans through the fine services of Outreach Specialist Lyn Singleton, MSW. He needs more people to help him reach and assist more veterans.

The heroes and heroines who staff the Veteran's Hospital on East 23rd Street in New York City are nameless and faceless on the street, in the subway and on a city bus. When they show up at The Veterans Hospital, they corral individuals carrying wounds of body and mind who are questioning: What was the purpose of it all then and what can possibly be as purposeful going forward? These soldiers of service are helping our veterans with the "let down".

VETERANS MOVING FORWARD — A WONDERFUL ORGANIZATION COMMITTED TO CREATING BETTER LIVES FOR DISABLED VETERANS

A friend of mine recently told me that everyone needs in life 1) purpose; 2) connectivity and 3) a good night's sleep! All three of these needs are hideously difficult to get when you need them the most.

Veterans Moving Forward is a not-for-profit organization introduced to me by my friend, John Prufeta, who is a founding board member and enthusiastic supporter. This organization helps disabled veterans connect by giving the veteran a highly-trained dog capable of performing many essential tasks. The veteran not only benefits from a remarkably smart "canine aide-de-camp" but gets love from "man's best friend".

Physically disabled veterans benefit tremendously from dogs trained to perform some 80 individual commands that help the veteran in their daily living, such as opening a door and retrieving medication, food and drink from the cabinet or refrigerator.

Veterans Moving Forward is made up of a staff of people dedicated to showing appreciation in a most useful way to citizens who have served our country and have paid a high price of reduced well-being to do so. This example of purpose in action is a poster child of leadership.

SHOW UP WHEN YOU ARE NEEDED

I was lying on the front hallway floor, having somehow fallen over backwards while climbing the steps in my house. Fortunately, I had not dropped my cell phone as I fell over about eight steps to collapse with a broken humerus bone on hitting the landing. I called my brother on my cell phone.

My brother called N.Y. 911 from Santa Fe, New Mexico. He told 911 to send an ambulance to me immediately. He then left his house in Santa Fe, New Mexico and flew to New York to be with me.

After I was released from the hospital, he accompanied me home and supervised my recovery for the next several days. Dr. Joel Schneider is both a surgeon and a pilot. More importantly, he is a leader because he stepped in to resolve my medical and emotional chaos when I most needed the help. It is said that 90% of success is showing up. Leaders show up.

CREATE A TRIBUTE

Romy Newman Cosmaciuc adored her stepfather, Henry E. Kates. My husband, Henry (Hank) E. Kates, adored Romy. I know Romy greatly misses her stepfather, who passed away four years ago.

I was, however, delightfully surprised when Romy recently said to me, she wanted me to react to an idea she had. She said she wanted to donate a bench, with a personalized plaque, in Central Park in honor of her stepfather. I could not have been more delighted to hear this idea.

The plaque on the bench is a reflection of Hank's constant puns. "Pun Last Time" is engraved on the plaque.

This act powerfully describes leadership behavior: Romy created everlasting recognition of her appreciation for Henry E. Kates.

To our beloved Hank,
Here's to you... pun last time.
Pamela, Romy, Bogdan,
Mary and Ted

Romy was able to channel her profound sense of loss into a charitable gift that would allow a forever tribute to her stepfather.

A LEADER KNOWS THERE CAN BE A BETTER WAY

Agnes Plonski has a number of jobs and responsibilities. One job responsibility she does NOT have is taking care of Mandarin Joey, my treasured Shih Tzu, on weekends and holidays. However, I was compelled to call Agnes on a recent holiday weekend. Why? I was on my second day of a hunger strike of this most loved canine. I was beside myself. I had fed him his favorite oven roasted white chicken meat, cut into small pieces and had absolutely no success in getting Mandarin to even look at it.

I know, I thought, what dog doesn't like hamburgers? I sizzled on the grill a nice juicy burger and fed it to Mandarin. He put his tail down and walked into the other room. I tried feeding him his favorite dog treats. Although Mandarin always joins me when he hears me opening the jar of treats, he came nowhere near the dog treats. I was distraught, I was befuddled. I wanted this otherwise very healthy dog to eat. I could not imagine what was going on. Was he angry at me? Had he gone on a diet and not shared this information with me? Did he dislike my choice of television programs to watch?

I could stand it no longer. I picked up the phone and called Agnes. She joined me and I explained to her all my various efforts. She reached into her pocket and said "I think I have the trick. Mandarin usually likes an appetizer before his entrée. Let's see if that works. He really likes pasta as a first course."

Agnes was correct. In moments, Mandarin gobbled down first the pasta and then the roasted chicken.

I wanted to eat the same thing myself.

LEADERS SEE THE OPPORTUNITY NO ONE ELSE SEES

My son, Theodore Ross Newman, recently called me and said, "I just had lunch with a friend of mine. He has started a business. I think you could help my friend's business go and grow."

Ted's friend has a business that sells a service unlike anything I know about. Yet, when I met Ted's friend, both of us could see where and how I could be useful.

I called Ted up and said to him: "Ted, how did you even think this might work?"

"Oh", he said, "I watch you do your work. I thought your skills would be appreciated by my friend."

Ted's vision is the vision of a leader. He can see what no one else sees at all.

USE TACT

Oddly, I see very little written about the importance of tact being used when dealing with other people. We all can think of moments when: 1) someone failed to speak tactfully to us and/or 2) we failed to speak tactfully to them.

Someone who could write a book (and give a course) on tact is Sari Rudmann. I am astounded at her capacity to subtlty get a message across to me.

When she doesn't like what I have written in an email, she gives it back to me with a word on top that says "Draft." When she sees I am worried about something, she tells me how she respects my concerns, yet she admonishes my fears. She builds into my schedule time to get ready for what I need to do and makes sure I use that time to get ready.

Tact is elegance defined. Sari is 100% tact.

LEADERS IMPROVE THE WORLD

I participated in a phone conversation today with an entrepreneur named Adam Treiser. The founder and CEO of Arjuna Solutions – **ExactAsk**. Adam Treiser has figured out how an algorithm can help fundraisers better realize donor lifetime value.

Making a new business requires leadership skills galore. An entrepreneur, such as Adam, has to convince people that their new concept is useful and that it works. People are naturally skeptical so an entrepreneur has to be able to "lead" an audience to believing his or her concept will improve the world and is, therefore, needed by the world. The entrepreneur has to be an effective champion of a new idea. A leader entrepreneur needs to be able to articulate their business model in a clear way and in a limited amount of time. The entrepreneur needs solid facts about the product's relevancy at their disposal.

An entrepreneurial leader needs to create believers who are willing to invest in the skill sets of the entrepreneur. An entrepreneurial leader has to be a potent force.

ONE FOOT IN FRONT OF THE OTHER

When I agreed to spend a few days visiting the University of South Carolina, it sounded like a nice idea. Moreover, it was an easy request to say "yes" to because the date for the visit was over six months away.

Six months flew by. Now, it was the night before I had to leave, and the trip seemed overwhelming to me because:

- I had too much work to do at home.

- I couldn't remember, or fathom, why I wanted to learn more about the University of South Carolina.

- The flights were early in the morning and required a layover in the Atlanta Airport.

By just putting "one foot in front of the other", I launched the trip. Looking back, the visit was not only easy to execute, but was a highly satisfying and a memorable event. Had I not taken this trip, I would:

- Never have seen a rare book collection of incredible importance.

- Not have had the enjoyable experience of teaching business school students at the Darla Moore School of Business.

- Have missed a side trip to Charleston, SC where I caught up with my dear friend Lou Hammond.

One foot in front of the other is the only way to take a trip, compete in a marathon and improve our society.

RELY ON TRAINING AND ACT ON THAT TRAINING

At a sad recent event in San Diego, a possibly deranged individual opened fire on parishioners in a synagogue. One parishioner, an Army trained individual, Oscar Stewart, grabbed a revolver from a drawer and pointed it at the active shooter. The active shooter fled from the synagogue as Stewart, a border patrol officer, confronted him, likely reducing the amount of injury and death for all the parishioners. Stewart's quick, decisive action reflected, he said, his training which is to defend people when they are attacked.

He never paused to think of his own well-being. His bravery, his action, his know-how reflected genuine leadership.

LEADERS TEACH

What makes some people natural leaders is that they do not have to be told what to do or how to do it. One day, alone in my office, Sam Plonski came into the office and noticed total pandemonium was breaking loose. I could not figure out how to, simultaneously, get into a Zoom call, answer the office line, answer the cell phone and get to the front door where somone was ringing the doorbell.

In a matter of minutes, Sam had restructured my environment, so I had the ability to get on and off a Zoom call on my own; reduce distractions and conflict.

He made the work environment more manageable.

Sam taught me leaders see things other people never see and then fix them.

LEADERS "BREAK GLASS"

There is an element of fear that prevents people from doing. I recently visited Israel. Every Israeli I met was ecstatic that our President had moved the U.S. Embassy from Tel Aviv to Jerusalem, which is the seat of government for Israel. What I could determine is that at least four previous Presidents supported moving the U.S. Embassy to Jerusalem but never actually did it as they had feared backlash. There was relatively little backlash. There were almost no demonstrations against the move. There was little press coverage critical of the move. Why had it taken decades to get a quite obvious thing done? This obvious correction did not cause a war, create strife, or reduce respect for Palestinians and Israelis.

The logical decision was an act of courage that no other President felt comfortable implementing.

RESTRUCTURE THE PARADIGM

It is, of course, an adjustment to be dating at this age. Since my husband passed away, I have entered into a set of evenings I have not experienced since I was in my very early twenties.

One of the revelations of dating is the need to figure out, and figure out quickly, the biorhythms of the date. For example, I recently went out on a double date. The other couple was hosting the evening at a very nice Parisian-styled bistro.

The waitress gave us the daily specials and then asked for our order. She directed the query to me. Not sure of the hosts' style of dining, I turned to the hostess and politely inquired, "Before we order, can you advise me if you are ordering an appetizer or just an entrée?"

"Dear: Whatever you like! Order whatever you like!", she replied. Buoyed by these effervescent words, I proceeded to order (as I customarily do) an appetizer and an entrée. Much to my disbelief, my hostess, host and date then proceeded to order only an entrée.

I felt duped and deceived. I felt piggish. I felt defensive. Why had no one either out of courtesy ordered an appetizer or had correctly guided me before I had ordered?

The offending tuna tartare appetizer arrived in good order. As I knew would be the case, I had created an extra discordant note in a simple musical score. All eyes fell on my tuna tartare while their plates remained naked. I was going to have to swallow this appetizer while everyone else had to wait for their entrée which had been slowed down from arriving by a good fifteen minutes while I was expected to enjoy the first course.

What to do? Exhibit leadership! How do you possibly exhibit leadership over having ordered an appetizer when no one else has? Restructure the paradigm.

In a flash of clarity, I reached first for my hostess' bread plate and without asking her or allowing her to demur, I lopped off 25% of my tuna tartare and put it on her bread and butter plate and presented it to her. In a series of swift and exacting moves, I repeated the exercise with my host and date's bread and butter plate.

Now, we all had an appetizer. The rhythm of the meal had been restored. All of us demolished our appetizers.

Opportunities for leadership moments abound wherever you are.

LEADERS ORGANIZE EVERYTHING

I have noted a common factor among leaders: Leaders tend to be very organized.

I recently read a wonderful book authored by former First Lady, Michelle Obama. While she pointed out that the President, Barrack Obama, was careless about leaving his socks and other things in unattended piles, he was fastidious about always having a private space where he could read, write, study and learn. His documents, in this space, were carefully placed for easy reference.

My daughter, her children, and I just visited Nashville, Tennessee for a chess tournament for my grandson. I observed how my daughter organized activities and time: She gave each child their own drawer for their clothes. She set up all toiletries in the bathroom so toothbrushes, toothpaste and brushes and combs could be effortlessly accessed. Even my nine-year-old grandson, Zachary, happily announced what our morning schedule should be and in doing so suggested an early lunch to accommodate the one-hour change in time from New York.

Leaders create an environment around them that reduces chaos. Leaders look to reduce friction in the system. Leaders make it a point to:

- Arrive early.

- Conduct a pilot of the excursion.

- Install back up plans and systems.

- Have an agenda.

THE NEEDS OF OTHERS COME BEFORE YOUR OWN

Procter & Gamble (P&G) CEO, Bob McDonald, points out in the book _The Story of Purpose_ by Joey Reiman that _"West Point taught me that character is the most important trait of a leader. I define character as always putting the needs of the organization above your own."_

PAINT A VIVID IMAGE OF SOME PLACE YOU WANT TO GO

Brigadier General Pete Dawkins delivered a wonderful presentation at the Metropolitan Club in New York City on February 11th, 2020.

General Dawkins won the Heisman Trophy at West Point. He studied at Oxford University. He received his Ph.D. from Princeton University. His courage on the battlefield made him a four-star general in the Army.

As successful as Pete was in academia, sports and the military, he also is a successful business executive, currently working for Virtu.

General Dawkins described leadership as the individual who displays vision, competence, will, character and trust. He pointed out that a leader paints a vivid image of some place to which you want to go.

LEADERS SEEM TO BE ABLE TO WORK AT A FASTER PACE

Angela Ritz is an individual I have always seen to be super organized. She is responsive and she is kind. She knows how to help. A skill set of hers I had not seen until the Coronavirus Pandemic, was her incredible ability to triple her workload and act on it with extraordinary velocity. You could see that she was in fifth gear. I cannot think that she was getting too much sleep.

Leaders seem to have the ability to move into high gear and do an enormous amount of work in a very short period of time.

That's Angela Ritz!

LEADERS ARE VISIONARIES

Chuck Stetson is a visionary who sees a world where obesity disappears; the onset of Alzheimer's Disease is delayed by ten years and diabetes is largely preventable. Chuck has created a not for profit called *The Coalition for Better Health at Lower Cost,* which is dedicated to bringing about these objectives. He plans to get this mission achieved through communication, persuasion and measurement.

Not one day goes by that Chuck doesn't wake up fully committed to his objectives.

Chuck can envision something no one else can see. Chuck Stetson is a visionary.

LISTEN HARD

Ted Newman, my son, has a talent for knowing the times I call him when I really need him to listen to my thoughts and react to what I am saying. His ability to hear is a herculean talent. Leaders listen.

Rather than discounting whatever is unnerving me, Ted indicates he gets why the issue is bothering me. He points out why, he suspects, the worry will prove needless.

A rarer dimension of good listening is deployed by Ted. He follows up soon after the helpful call to see how things are going and to reaffirm positively.

I trust Ted's selfless listening skills. Moreover, I rely on them.

EPILOGUE

Usually, when we finish reading a book, we place it on a shelf. Possibly, we give it to a friend. Maybe, we refer to it once or twice after reading it.

Typically, the points made in a book fade away over time. This book, *Leadership is Doing*, is hopefully the beginning of heightened awareness and interest in cultivating leadership moments.

People read about the importance of exercise and then exercise. Likewise, people read about the importance of diet and often change their eating habits accordingly.

Upon studying stress management, people often get serious about Yoga.

Cultivating leadership capability is an undertaking worthwhile spending time on.

Focusing on leadership opportunities better enables us to see a moment for leadership when it is in front of us.

As time passes after reading this book, it might be useful to make a list of leadership moments you execute or observe.

1. _____

2. _____

3. _____

4. _____

5. _____

6. _____

7. _____

8. _____

9. _____

10. _____

This book began with the example of going to San Diego as an example of leadership being about doing. Traveling anywhere has been foreshortened by the reality that we are still in the midst of COVID-19 uncertainty.

We are seeing people we love less.

We have become trapped from doing because of our fears about the pandemic.

I believe in practicing leadership. Equipped with an

N95 mask and a plexiglass face shield, I decided to travel to San Diego to see my family. The airport and plane both allowed for easy social distancing.

I am, as I write these words, soaking up the joy of being with people I love as though they were rays of sunshine providing me Vitamin D.

Leadership Is Doing

CPSIA information can be obtained
at www.ICGtesting.com
Printed in the USA
LVHW011507040623
748851LV00027B/181/J